Scary Tales

Rhymes for Brave Children

For Raewyn, my superstar sister – JB
For Tai, a very special little ogre – DH

Thank you to all those who took the time to test drive our book. Your honest feedback has been invaluable.

Judi Billcliff is a crazy drama teacher and author. She visits schools entertaining children with her magical poetry performances.

Deborah Hinde is a good witch in disguise. She hangs out in her studio bringing stories to life with her magic brushes.

A catalogue of this book is available from the National Library of New Zealand.
ISBN: 978-0-473-48304-3

Published in 2019 by PictureBook Publishing
PO Box 455, Te Awamutu 3840, New Zealand.
www.picturebook.co.nz

Text © Judi Billcliff 2019 www.rainbowpoetry.co.nz
Illustrations © Deborah Hinde 2019 www.deborahhinde.com
The moral rights of the author and illustrator have been asserted.
This book is copyright. Except for the purposes of fair reviewing, no part of this publication may be reproduced or transmitted in any form or by any means, electronic or mechanical, including photocopying, recording or any information storage and retrieval system without permission in writing from the publisher.

Designed by Deborah Hinde
Edited by Sue Copsey www.suecopsey.com
Distributed in New Zealand by The Book Department Ltd. www.thebookdept.co.nz
Printed and bound in China by Asia Pacific Offset Ltd.

Scary Tales

Rhymes for Brave Children

Judi Billcliff and Deborah Hinde

PictureBook Publishing

Mary had a Little Ghost

Mary had a little ghost,
It followed her to school.
All the children screamed with fright,
"A ghost at school's not cool!"

Tai hid under the table,
Jack hid under the chair.
Rosie hid in the cupboard,
Kids hid everywhere!

He slid across the tables
And then he spilt the paint.
The teacher, Mrs Wiggle cried,
"Help! I'm going to faint!"

He tipped out all the pencils
And scribbled on the board.
When it came to being naughty
He'd win the top award.

Mary yelled at Little Ghost,
"Please stop! This isn't right!
You need to help us tidy up,
Not give my friends a fright!"

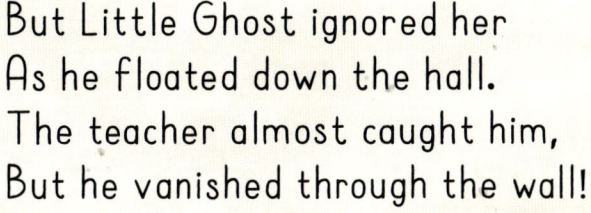

But Little Ghost ignored her
As he floated down the hall.
The teacher almost caught him,
But he vanished through the wall!

So if *you* have a little ghost,
Please don't bring it to school.
Screaming kids and all that mess,
Simply isn't cool!

Hector the Zombie Cat

Hector is a pussycat
Who comes alive at night.
He turns into a zombie
And gives everyone a fright.

He scares them in the buses,
He scares them in the trains,
Families driving in their cars
And folk in aeroplanes.

Hector doesn't mean them harm,
It's his idea of fun.
When the sun begins to rise,
His zombie day is done.

When your little pussycat
Runs off into the night,
He might just be a zombie,
Out giving folk a fright.

Werewolf to the Rescue

"Werewolf, werewolf,
Where have you been?"
"I've been to the castle
To visit the Queen."

"Tell me, oh werewolf,
Why were you there?"
"To rescue seven dwarves
Hiding under her chair!"

Sweet Treat

"Little goblin, little goblin, let me come in."
"Not by the wart on my chinny, chin, chin!"

"Little goblin, little goblin, please let me in."
"Not by the hairs on my thorny green skin!"

"Open the door, I've brought you a treat,
It's gooey, runny and delicious to eat."

He opened the door, *"Come in, take a seat."*
The ogre grinned ... then he ate him,
"Goblins sure do taste sweet!"

Frankie Loses his Britches

Little Frankie sat on a wall,
Little Frankie had a big fall.
He landed on a coven of witches
Who ran away with his brand-new britches!

Little Frankie hid behind a wall,
A passing mouse heard him call,
"Can you help me? Help me please!
I've lost my pants, I'm going to freeze!"

Little Frankie sat on a wall,
But little Frankie didn't fall.
He said, "I know what I can do,
I'll cover my bum with super glue!"

The Little Ghouls Party

If you go down to the park tonight
You're sure of a big surprise.
If you go down to the park tonight
You'll never believe your eyes.

For every ghoul that ever there was
Will gather there for certain
Because, tonight's the night
The ghouls are having a party.

Party time for little ghouls,
The playful little ghouls are having
A lot of fun tonight.
See them flying through the air,
Their shadows chase them
In the evening light.

Watch them having lots of fun,
Hear their happy laughter
Echo all around.
At eight o'clock their mummies and daddies
Will take them home to bed,
Because they're tired little grumpy ghouls.

Croonella Crombie and the Zombie

Croonella Crombie met a zombie
Walking to the fair.
Said Miss Crombie to the zombie,
"What will you do there?"
Said the zombie to Miss Crombie,
"I'll be giving folk a fright,
With terrifying shrieks and howls,
It'll be a fearsome night!"
Said Miss Crombie to the zombie,
"How very mean of you."
The zombie said, "Miss Crombie dear,
It's what we zombies do!"

Flying Witchypoo

Witchypoo flies her scooter
All around her cave,
Merrily, merrily, merrily, merrily,
Feeling very brave!

Witchypoo flies her scooter
Out into the sun,
Merrily, merrily, merrily, merrily,
Time to have some fun!

Witchypoo flies her scooter
Up and down the stream,
Scarily, scarily, scarily, scarily,
Making children scream!

Witchypoo flies her scooter
All around the lake,
Scarily, scarily, scarily, scarily,
Making children shake!

Witchypoo flies her scooter
On a stormy night,
Wibbly, wobbly, wibbly, wobbly –
She disappears from sight!

Liar, Liar

Augustus was a silly boy
Who found it fun to lie.
It made his mother quite upset,
She'd often ask him, "Why?"

"Why do you make up stories son?
You've become a liar!"
But still he thought it would be fun
To shout out, "Fire! Fire!"

As soon as he had said the words
The house rocked with a bang.
His worried mother rushed right in ...
And found he'd sprouted fangs!

"Your eyes are bloodshot!" gasped his mum,
"Your skin has gone all white.
I told you that you shouldn't lie
'Cos lying's never right!"

"I DON'T tell lies or porky pies!"
Said Augustus with a wail,
"I've never, ever told a lie!"
He grew a spiky tail.

Before his mother could reply,
There came a puff of smoke,
And standing in their kitchen was –
A wizardy looking bloke.

"Good evening young Augustus,
You've just run out of lies.
It's time you started learning
To be honest, kind and wise."

"You can't stop me!" Augustus teased,
Dancing round the floor.
So the wizard cast a magic spell ...
And Augustus spoke no more!

Sing a Song of Silliness

Sing a song of silliness
A saucepan full of grease.
A dozen naughty children
Were baked inside a quiche.

When the quiche was served up
The kids began to shout.
"That was such a slippery dish
It made us all fall out!"

The king was in his office
Talking on his phone.
The queen was in the bathroom
Sitting on her throne.

The cook was in the kitchen
Trying to make a quiche.
But had to make a stew instead
As she'd run out of grease!

My Dog Turned into a Vampire

My dog turned into a vampire,
It happened on Friday night.
I'd no idea what was going on,
But it gave me an awful fright.

The dog was sleeping on my knee
When he began to growl.
"What's the matter Hercules?"
He let out a mighty howl.

Suddenly, he was twice his size,
His eyes had turned blood red.
He'd grown a pair of pointy fangs,
And horns poked out his head.

His lip curled; he began to snarl,
And then he ate my mother!
My dad was next to disappear,
And then my smelly brother.

He ate my gran — boy, she was tough,
Granddad gave him a whack!
But Hercules ate him in one gulp,
Just like a morning snack!

He ate Hip and Hop our bunnies
And Candice our canary.
All our Mexican walking fish
And then our Great Aunt Mary!

Hercules was on a roll,
He devoured our neighbour Pat,
Who happened to be holding tight
His brand-new ginger cat.

I kept on calling out to him,
"Hercules, stop! No more!
You can't keep eating everyone."
He bolted out the door.

Hercules lay down with a groan,
His belly overloaded.
He let out one almighty burp,
Then Hercules

exPloded!

I got a new pup yesterday,
I thought I'd call him Stan.
The only meat that Stan will eat,
Is what comes in a can!

What Are Little Ogres Made Of?

What are little ogres made of?
What are little ogres made of?
Grit and grime
And gooey slime,
That's what little ogres are made of.

What are little vampires made of?
What are little vampires made of?
Blood and bones
And slimy stones,
That's what little vampires are made of.

What are little witches made of?
What are little witches made of?
Fingernails
And maggots' tails,
That's what little witches are made of.

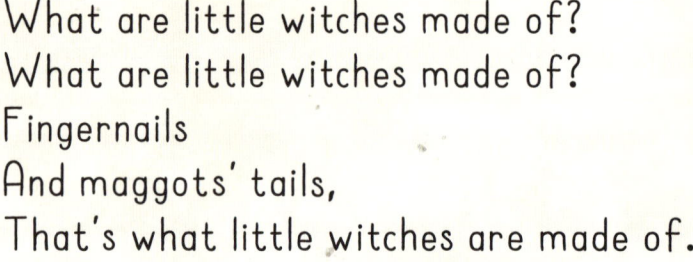

What are little goblins made of?
What are little goblins made of?
Grungy gunk
And pickled skunk,
That's what little goblins are made of.

Gloria Glitter

Gloria Glitter was a quirky critter
Who liked to eat lemons
And anything bitter!
After bathing in broth
She turned into a goth
And posted her photo on twitter!

Old Count Dracula had a Vault

Old Count Dracula had a vault, A E I O U.
And in that vault he had some *kids!* A E I O U.
With a boy hiding here,
And a girl huddling there,
Here a child,
There a child,
Screaming, "Get us out of here!"
Old Count Dracula had a vault, A E I O U.

Old Count Dracula had a vault, A E I O U.
And in that vault he had some *bats!* A E I O U.
With a bat flying here,
And a bat flapping there,
Here a bat,
There a bat,
Giving everyone a scare!
Old Count Dracula had a vault, A E I O U.

Old Count Dracula had a vault, A E I O U.
And in that vault he had some *bugs!* A E I O U.
With a bug creeping here,
And a bug crawling there,
Here a bug,
There a bug,
Bugs scuttling everywhere!
Old Count Dracula had a vault, A E I O U.

Old Count Dracula had a vault, A E I O U.
And in that vault he had some *zombies!* A E I O U.
With a zombie moaning here,
And a zombie groaning there,
Here a zombie,
There a zombie,
Zombies roaming everywhere.
Old Count Dracula had a vault, A E I O U.

Are you going to help the children escape?
Everyone get ready.
Inside we go ... shhh,
Opening the vault door.
Uh oh, here comes Count Dracula. Three, two, one ...
Run kids, RUN!

Little Miss Muffet

Little Miss Muffet
Sat on her tuffet,
Eating her eggs on toast.
Along came a weevil
Who looked rather evil,
"Ah, eggs are what I love most!"

Weevil was shocked
As he sat on his rock,
And heard Miss Muffet cry,
"You're not having mine,
So don't start to whine
Or I'll cook you up in a pie!"

Little Miss Muffet
Sat on her tuffet,
Eating her eggs on toast.
A sneaky old grasshopper
Said, "I will stop her
As toast is what I love most."

Grasshopper declared,
"Your toast will be shared!"
But little Miss M said, "It won't!
Don't you dare moan,
You go make your own,
Or I'll turn you into a roast!"

Who's the Scariest?

"Mirror, mirror, on the wall,
Who's the scariest of them all?"
"It's always been you my goblin queen,
You're the scariest one I've seen.
Your pointy ears, your rough green skin,
Your large hooked nose, your spiky chin.
Your popping eyes, so bright and yellow,
The way you scream, the way you bellow.
But today I saw a human being,
And couldn't believe what I was seeing.
Her skin so pale, her lips so red,
A sparkling tiara on her head.
The most hideous creature I've ever seen,
Even more frightful than you, my queen."
"Tell me who. That can't be right!"
"I'm told she's known as ... Snow White."
"Mirror, mirror, on the wall,
Who's the scariest of them all?"
"I cannot lie, I must be true,
Snow White, my queen, is scarier than you!"

The Witch with a Twitch

Little Bo Peep took her sheep
To drink at the farmer's pond.
She met an old witch
Who had a bad twitch
And a dodgy-looking wand!

"Those tasty sheep will fall asleep,
The moment I cast my spell!
I'll be a winner,
They'll be my dinner,"
And down on the grass they fell.

Little Bo Peep began to weep
As she ran back down the lane.
She found Farmer Fred
Who angrily said,
"Not that pesky witch again!"

Little Bo Peep left her sheep
For Farmer Fred to save.
She sat on her tush
Under a bush
Not feeling very brave.

Farmer Fred, he found that witch
And broke her dodgy wand.
The sheep woke up,
They asked, "Wassup?"
Then chased her into the pond.

Scary Mary

Scary Mary quite contrary
How does your garden grow?
With wailing moans
And rattling bones
All hanging in a row.

Scary Mary quite contrary
How does your garden grow?
With screeching howls
And hooting owls
All sitting in a row.

Scary Mary, quite contrary
How does your garden grow?
With werewolves and witches
And goblins in ditches
And skeletons all in a row.

Werewolves and owls all sing and dance,
While goblins hide underground.
The witches are busy
Casting their spells,
But the skeletons just hang around.

The Strangest Time

There's a time when birds swim upside down,
When goldfish fly all through the town.
When dogs meow and cats bark
But it only happens after dark.

When wolves cluck and chickens howl
When bears buzz and bees growl.
When frogs go *hiss*, and snakes leap
But it only happens when you sleep.

When monkeys moo and cows shriek
When mice chirp and crickets squeak.
When crocs jump and roos bite
But it only happens late at night.

When lambs oink and piglets bleat
And giraffes run wild along the street.
It's the strangest thing I've ever seen
But it only happens on Halloween!

Did you know?

We've been busy researching facts for you, but what Google says isn't always true!

Sheep can see what's behind them without having to turn their heads, but they can't see things right in front of them. Someone should invent glasses for sheep!
In New Zealand there are 5.6 sheep for every person. That's a lot of sheep!

Bats Have you heard the saying 'blind as a bat?' Well, guess what? Bats actually have good eyesight. To help them see in the dark, they use a special skill called echolocation. A bat will make a noise, then wait for the echo to bounce back off an object. If there's no echo they know it's safe to fly forward. They can tell how far away an object is by how quickly the sound bounces back to them.
Bats must be very good at playing hide and seek!

Cats and dogs can see ultraviolet light. So when your pet's acting crazy, it could be because they can see something you can't. It might even be a ghost!
There's no record anywhere of a human having been hurt by a ghost. Phew!

A hippopotamus's bite is as dangerous as a lion's. A hippo can bite an unsuspecting human in half in one go. Hippos are found in Africa.

Owls don't have eyeballs, like humans. They can't roll their eyes like we can; they have to turn their head to look around.
I wonder what an owl does when his mother tells him he has to go to bed?
A group of owls is called a parliament. What a hoot!

Spiders have brains, but they aren't like human brains. The smaller the spider, the bigger the brain. Believe it or not, some small spiders' brains are so large they spill into their legs!
Spiders have a natural wetsuit, as the hairs on their legs are water-repellent. This is why they can float.
The world's most venomous spider is Australia's male funnel-web.
The majority of tarantulas are found in South America, where the male of one species dances to impress his girlfriends. While tarantulas might look scary, they're harmless to humans.

Grasshoppers existed before dinosaurs, which makes them older than your grandparents!
A grasshopper's hind legs act like miniature catapults, which is why they can jump so far.
Grasshoppers are eaten all over the world, and are a popular after-school snack in some countries, like Thailand and Japan. There's even a grasshopper farm in Israel. Hop on over!

Rats clean themselves many times each day. Imagine having to have a bath every time you ate. Rats have an excellent sense of smell. They can be trained to detect illnesses in humans. Quite a few cities in the world have more rats than people. I wonder who counts the rats!

Witches in stories are nearly always mean and nasty. They wear dark colours, have warts on their pointy noses, and fly around on broomsticks. But the ancient Greeks and Romans appreciated good witches, as they believed they could make sick people well, help crops grow, and protect them from evil spirits or disasters like floods.

Zombies don't exist, but kids love to read and write about them. The word 'zombi' was first used in Haiti, a country in Central America, where legend has it that a sorcerer called Bokor used black magic to bring people back to life.

Ghouls are mythical (made-up) creatures that first appeared in Arabian folklore. They were said to live in creepy, uninhabited places.

Goblins are also mythical. Some people believe they are mischievous fairies, while others think they are grotesque, evil, greedy monsters. Whatever they are, we can all agree goblins are troublemakers who possess magical powers.

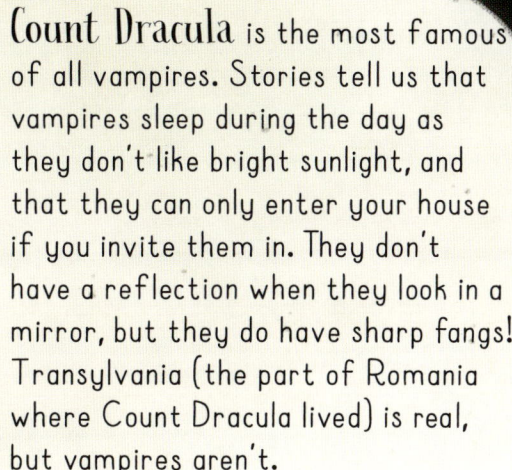

Count Dracula is the most famous of all vampires. Stories tell us that vampires sleep during the day as they don't like bright sunlight, and that they can only enter your house if you invite them in. They don't have a reflection when they look in a mirror, but they do have sharp fangs! Transylvania (the part of Romania where Count Dracula lived) is real, but vampires aren't.

Halloween grew out of an ancient festival celebrated by a people called the Celts. They celebrated New Year on 1 November, and believed that on the last day of October, spirits roamed the earth. They would dress up in costumes, believing this would frighten them away. They would also leave food at the edge of the town, hoping the roaming spirits would eat it instead of raiding their homes.

As people emigrated to America, a new tradition was created there. Now children all over the world dress up for Halloween and visit houses for 'trick-or-treating.'

Ghastly Jokes

Q: What do you call a goblin with a broken foot?
A: A hobblin' goblin!

Q: How do ghosts wash their hair?
A: With shamboo!

Q: What does a witch use to do her hair?
A: Scarespray!

Q: What happens when a vampire goes out in the snow?
A: He gets frost bite!

Q: Where do baby ghosts go during the day?
A: Dayscare centres!

Q: What is a monster's favourite dessert?
A: Icecream!

Q: What do ghosts do when they get hurt?
A: They cry 'Boo hoo!'

Activities

1. Cut two eye holes in an old sheet and you've got the easiest Halloween costume ever. Becoming a real ghost might take a bit more time.

2. One person sits on a chair in the middle of the room and closes their eyes. Others have to touch them with something (e.g. a piece of rope, a wand, slime) and the person on the chair tries to guess what it is.

3. One person sits on a chair. Others take turns to approach them saying, 'I am a scary ghost!' They can pull a scary face, use a silly voice, or move in a ghostlike way. The object is to make the person on the chair laugh. If they laugh, someone else has a turn on the chair. If they keep a straight face, they get another turn. Try other greetings like, 'I'm a wailing witch,' or, 'I'm a moaning monster.' You can moan or wail as you say who you are.

4. Create a scary, eerie, treasure hunt for your friends or family.

5. Play 'Pin The Tail On The Black Cat' (but not on a real one!) Draw and paint your own black cat and cut out some tail shapes.

6. Have fun saying this tongue twister:
'Which witch was a wicked witch, and which witch is a twitchy witch.'
Make up your own fun tongue twister.

7. How many words can you make out of the letters in the word SUPERSTITION?
   10 words – well done   20 words – excellent
   50 words – brilliant   100 words – outstanding achievement
   If you can find some 8 or 9 letter words – a word champion.

8. Have fun with spells. Try this one with your friends.
"Abracadabra binkety boo. I am a . . . . . (e.g. a naughty goblin) What are you?"
Maybe you could have fun acting out who or what you are.